10K Boss

The Power of Everyday Entrepreneurialism

Compiled and Edited by
Suzi Chen PhD

First published in Australia in 2017 by
NOTONOS GLOBAL PTY LTD

PO Box 1097 Glen Waverley
Victoria 3150 Australia

www.notonos.com
editorialteam@notonos.com

Copyright © Suzi Chen and Notonos Global, 2017

Printed and bound in Australia

The moral right of the authors has been asserted.

All rights reserved. Without limiting the rights under copyright reserved above, no part of this publication may be reproduced, stored or introduced into a retrieval system, or transmitted, in any form or by any means (electronic, mechanical, photocopying, recoding or otherwise), without the prior written permission of both the copyright owner and the publisher of this book.

ISBN 978 0 6481357 0 8 (paperback)
ISBN 978 0 6481357 1 5 (eBook)

National Library of Australia Cataloguing-in-Publication entry

Title: 10K boss : the power of everyday entrepreneurialism / compiled and edited by Suzi Chen PhD; contributing authors: Nic Henry Jones, Caroline Carswell and Andrew Constantine.

ISBN: 9780648135708 (paperback)
ISBN: 978 0 6481357 1 5 (eBook)

Subjects: Entrepreneurship--Australia.
Business people--Australia.
Success in business.

Other Creators/Contributors:
Chen, Suzi, compiler, editor.
Jones, Nic Henry, author.
Carswell, Caroline, author.
Constantine, Andrew, author.

~

Dedicated to all the everyday entrepreneurs out there who fight a fearless fight while taking on a meaningful journey.

~

Contents

PREFACE ix

PART I

What Success? I Had No Idea What Would
Unfold 11

PART II

A Non-Prescribed Journey 29

PART III

Mr Economics, I Have Made It! 53

Preface

"Entrepreneur" has become a buzzword. Many dream to be one, yet only a few truly succeed.

The term *entrepreneur* is often associated with individuals known for extraordinary achievements. While the likes of Sir Richard Branson and Chris Guillebeau are inspirational and powerful examples of entrepreneurialism, we should not forget that the entrepreneurial spirit is often closer to home. And once upon a time, Sir Richard Branson started out just like our everyday entrepreneurs.

Everyday entrepreneurs are those of us who have a dream and dare to take actions to make the dream come true. They are not that different from you and I except for their strong conviction, fearless attitude to make things happen and the willingness to break away from the day to day work grind that we are often part of.

It is the stories of these everyday entrepreneurs that we want to share with our readers, and hence the birth of the 10K Boss: the Power of Everyday Entrepreneurialism Book Project.

Why 10K?

The arbitrary figure was chosen to symbolise the challenges that everyday entrepreneurs face, particularly in the area of finance management and their admirable perseverance and creative ability to deliver in spite of challenges.

In this book, we share the stories of 3 everyday entrepreneurs from different industry sectors. Each story comes with its unique ambition and difficulties, but all share the unwavering strength and true grit to make it happen. Let these stories inspire you and even better, set you in motion for your own everyday entrepreneurial journey.

After all, we do live in a world of opportunities.

Suzi Chen (PhD)
Editor

PART 1

10K BOSS

WHAT SUCCESS? I HAD NO IDEA WHAT WOULD UNFOLD.

NIC HENRY JONES
Market Me Marketing

"Success is doing what you want to do, when you want, where you want, with whom you want, as much as you want."

- Anthony Robbins

I suppose I had always had a desire to run my own business and to work for myself. I'd run a few hobby businesses and managed to earn enough money to get a tax write-off for a few years. In reality, those business adventures were a lesson-learning experience rather than a viable business operation. I learned so much with those hobby businesses that when I started Market Me Marketing, I nailed it first time around.

At the age of 31, I found myself in the industry I now work in. At the time, I had a simple goal. I wanted to make 25 dollars an hour from home around my kids. I had no idea what would unfold.

Looking back now, I can see that I was really undervaluing myself and my contribution to the world by playing small.

The picture today tells a different story.

~

It was April 2010. My twin boys were only 9 months old and brands were just starting to use Facebook for business. It was back in the day when welcome pages were one of the initial ways brands could visually get across what they do in less than 10 seconds.

Businesses were excited about how Facebook, as a platform, could "get the word out" and connect with customers in a way that a website on its own couldn not. There was a tremendous opportunity to build brand awareness using Facebook, growing a following and connecting with people on a more personal level.

Posting up-to-date information and talking to

customers online generated a new sense of energy in the business world. This phenomenon had a name and it was called digital marketing. It was all new back then, and I was right in the middle of it. My curiosity not only saw me dabbling in Facebook, it also helped me spot great business marketing opportunities.

I noticed that while Facebook was becoming popular, many business owners did not quite understand it and certainly were not using it at its best.

But I could!

Like a beacon in the dark, I could easily identify the challenges that businesses were facing with Facebook. Better still, I also had a creative solution for these challenges. My mind worked in such a way that I could simplify things and pull the most important information together for others, so people could be empowered instead of being confused.

So I started at $25 an hour, creating welcome pages for brands on Facebook.

This was the beginning of my business journey.

~

I was a stay-at-home mother with 3 children on little budget. Wait, scrap that! Actually, I had no budget.

What I had was time and a desire to learn and allow my business to evolve over time.

I may be bias, but the best name for a marketing company came to me on one of those "startup" mind racing idea days. I literally was throwing around ideas for business names and out of nowhere came Market Me Marketing. Being sleep deprived at the time, I didn't realise what an incredible name it was until someone pointed it out to me at a later date.

Thinking back, this was a perfect example demonstrating how often we over think in business. We can easily get lost in a myriad of ideas, if not careful. Just like how I almost missed my perfect company name.

Contrary to most start-ups, I did not necessarily anticipate significant growth in the beginning. My goal was to earn $25 an hour from home to supplement our income. I figured earning that amount without having to leave home or put kids in full-time childcare would be awesome. So instead of finding money and energy to invest in a website, I decided I would just dive straight in and work the business, website or not. I initially used Facebook to share my portfolio with others and to educate and connect with people. I also used the opportunity to share the types of things I thought were working on Facebook and what Market Me Marketing could do to help.

Several years later, I finally built my website to help with my digital presence. Even then it was an ever evolving process. I had started out with an initial logo and colour scheme that I liked, just to get me off the ground. The brown and pink creation was scrapped 2 years later as I re-branded when finance became available, and when I had a more concrete idea where my business was going. As my business continued to grow, I came to learn one of my most important lessons in business - expect the unexpected and evolve as you go.

Instead of waiting for everything to line up, I learned to dive in, adapt and capture the opportunity right there and then.

~

Website-less did not bother me, because I had a strategy. I started a Facebook Page and built my first thousand Facebook followers by connecting with people on their business page with a non-salesy "great to meetyou, feel free to connect" message. In this self-introductory message, I explained to others what I loved about their business page and invited them to connect with me. It was not spammy or salesy, rather a digital form of networking.

I spent some time connecting with 10 to 20 new businesses each day, and my own following began to grow over time. I invested in my followers by providing quality content and interesting links and tips to help other businesses grow. I put an emphasis on genuinely interacting with my followers.

This strategy served me well as I have created many lasting connections on Facebook - connections that have turned into long term clients, business friends and avid followers.

These meaningful connections opened the door of opportunities.

Fearless in Pursuing Opportunities

I virtually met a copywriter on a Facebook Page who was starting out just like me. We became business friends and supported each other on our entrepreneurial journey, attending events together, promoting each other and picking each other up when the going got tough.

The business relationship grew and eventually it turned into collaboration. We now run a Digital

Collective together, offering a complete website and copywriting service.

Opportunities continued to present themselves while I implemented my "digital networking" strategy.

I remember connecting with another interesting business through Facebook Page. To my amazement, only 2 hours after the initial connection, I was already on the phone with its business owner, discussing how my business could potentially help remedy a crisis situation. As it turned out, their social media guru had quit and they had no replacement to lead the way forward.

I was given this opportunity to provide a quote, and by 9 am the next morning I had signed up an on-going client that was worth $400 each month. I continued to service this client for the next 2 years until the business changed hands. My service was recommended to the next business owner. This gave me a taste of the power of world of mouth marketing in the business world.

People are often surprised by the number of opportunities that come my way. I truly believe it is because I have chosen to foster an environment where opportunities can flourish. I have chosen to allow my business to evolve. I'm not bogged down into the way it has to be. I am open to my business growing in the direction of natural flows.

~

In 2011, I did exactly that – I evolved. I decided I would offer free training as a way of helping others make the most of Facebook.

Training was always a passion. I saw delivering webinars and educating business owners about how to use Facebook effectively a perfect way to help build a community, my profile and my business.

Needless to say, the first attempt was nerve-racking. I spent weeks putting my first webinar together and countless hours practicing the delivery of it. Little did I know that this webinar would become and continue to be one of my key lead generation tools.

It turned out that people enjoyed seeing me in action and I repeatedly ran this webinar at 8 pm every month for about 18 months. The biggest audience I ever had with this particular webinar was 94 people from across the country. In 1 hour, webinar participants could clearly learn how to move their business forward on social media with tips, hints and simple strategies. This was a useful lead generation strategy. I always had clients and requests in my inbox after webinar training.

I later added workshops into my business offering, but I will always remember how my desire to evolve catapulted me into this amazing opportunity.

Persistence and Determination

Circumstances are never perfect and life happens. The best thing you can do is to strive for better and keep moving forward with persistence and determination at your best pace, plus some.

Like many business owners, I found the first year of my business particularly difficult. Not only did I have twin boys to look after, my marriage was not going well, and I was also extremely unwell. I was diagnosed with sarcoidosis, an inflammatory disease that attacks multiple organs in the body.

As a result of it, I had great trouble breathing and speaking without coughing. There were days I had to schedule phone calls with clients from bed.

I was that sick that eventually I was admitted to a hospital for a week, at 51 kg, with the sarcoid, pneumonia and another infection. It took me 12 months to recover from this health crisis, but I never stopped working on my business.

Life happens, and you soldier on.

So I did.

I knew running a business and looking after 3 children including 2 new born twin boys was not going to be easy. So I learned to perfect my organisational skills, and I implemented a strict routine with my twin boys. In a way, this was my coping mechanism. I wasn't sure how else to get through with my twin boys during this difficult time, business or no business.

So imagine this:

The twins would go to bed at 7 pm.
I rested for 40 minutes.
Regardless of how I felt, I would get up at 7.40 pm and be ready for my webinar.
I then stayed energetic and vibrant for an hour, getting people excited about the possibilities of Facebook.
I then collapsed into bed at 9 pm for one hour before next feeds.

And I repeated this again next time around.

It was crazy. At times I wondered if it was all worth it. Looking back, every single bit of pushing through was worth it. Some days I could only do the basics, and other times I was pumping out development projects like there was no tomorrow.

Circumstances are never perfect. Life happens, both good and bad. The truth is there will always be something going on in life that could stop us from achieving our goals. The key is to focus on why you are running a business and keep moving.

Lifelong Learner

My journey as a self-taught marketer began in April 2010. It was a bold move, and it was incredibly satisfying. Everything was new, and the unknown became the accepted norm.

I decided early on that nothing was too hard and that if I did not know how to do something, I would just go and learn. If a client wanted information on something that I did not have on hand, I would go and find out and learn how to do it. No excuses and no limits.

I adopted a learn-and-earn model that essentially positioned my business as a lifesaver to our clients. It is a win-win situation.

As a solopreneur, I have come to realise the importance of learning. The more you learn, the greater your confidence, the greater your skills, the more you can offer and the more you can earn.

WordPress-based web design and maintenance is now 40% of our business revenue, but none of my clients know how much I disliked WordPress when I first started my business.

It might seem a little conflicting, but I really don't like technology much! I found WordPress hard to understand and I had my share of tears while trying to troubleshoot (different landscape today). It was always a challenge. There were times I wished I could avoid using WordPress all together. It wasn't until clients started asking for WordPress services that I realised I really had to learn it.

Today WordPress web design and maintenance contributes significantly to Market Me Marketing's business growth.

As my business expands, so does my team. This learn-and-earn model continues to motivate us and reminds us not to be limited by the "this is how we have always done it" mentality, but to keep pushing through into new learnings to strengthen our offering.

Although I did not attend university, I learned to grow my business intuitively. I had chosen to build into my skill set eagerness to learn, flexibility, creativity, dependability, vision and resourcefulness. These qualities form the foundations of my marketing company and account for a big portion of our success. These are also the attributes that I look for when recruiting team members.

Open Doors Through Collaborations

I was asked to do a 10-minute social media talk at a networking event in 2010. I was sick as a dog that day, but decided I would push through and go. I met one of my long-term clients, a Registered Training Organisation, that day who would later add another dimension to Market Me Marketing.

I ended up collaborating with this particular client and accepting a guest speaking invitation at their accredited courses, which they were rolling out in South Australia. I really enjoyed my one hour guest appearance with this client, speaking all things social media. This little gig gave me a taste of being a trainer and I rediscovered training others was a lifelong passion of mine.

This short gig turned into something bigger. I was asked by the same client if I would consider becoming a fully qualified trainer instead of just being a guest speaker. I jumped at the opportunity, because I knew that in the end this would help me further achieve my goals and give opportunity for my passion.

As I became more confident, I started rolling out my own non-accredited training, writing my own workshops and webinars. I was even brave enough to schedule my online training across the year and in different regions.

Designing and delivering webinars was not an easy task, but I trusted my instinct that webinars were a great way to educate people on a variety of things while building my industry credibility and generating leads. I knew I was on the right path when I could walk away with a few leads every time I ran a webinar. This training initiative also provided a level of personal satisfaction as I relished the chance to give back to others.

While other marketing companies and business owners have been spending money advertising on Google or relying on other paid marketing strategies, I have simply chosen to work creatively, utilise word of mouth marketing and stay tuned for opportunities through collaborations.

Collaboration has revolutionised my business.

It turns out helping others to achieve their goals has been the vehicle for me to achieve further success in my business and my own goals.

Self-Doubt Stops Dreams from Coming True

Self-doubt is a common stumbling block for anyone who has a dream. I was no different. The biggest thing that held me back really was not believing in myself enough.

When I started Market Me Marketing, I really didn't have the support of those closest to me. Although I was strong enough to filter out other people's opinions and embarked on my journey, deep inside it was a tough gig.

Unbelievably, it took me a good 5 years to build up self-confidence and actually believe that I was qualified enough by experience. I also had to learn to celebrate the person I have become for the success I had achieved.

If I could turn back time, I would have my conviction strong knowing that my passion, my yearning for learning, my creativity and my common sense can really stand on their own in many ways. I know that because Market Me Marketing has made it.

In just under 7 years in business, Market Me Marketing has gone from zero followers, no skills, no influence, $25 per hour Welcome Page Designs and free webinars to over 7,500 followers on Facebook, over 2,000 followers on Instagram and more on the other social media channels.

People across Australia now know who we are and what we do. We are the digital marketing experts that Councils and Regional Development Officers call on to help roll out their regional training.

We have achieved financial success and hit our 6

figure goal; something that I did not ever imagine I would achieve initially.

In 2017, my business has come to a point where I now need to dream again, to risk again and to evolve again. But this time around, I have a team who I can grow with. I'm so excited by what the next 10 years will hold for Market Me Marketing and the impact that, I, as the Director will be able to have, with my team right behind me.

About Nic Henry Jones

Nic Henry Jones is the Creator, Director and Senior Digital Media Strategist behind Market Me Marketing Australia.

In 2010, Nic dived into the solopreneur world wanting to use her creative skills on something and with the ambition to earning $25 an hour while staying at home to look after her twin newborns and daughter.

Today the self-taught and experience-based creative digital marketer leads a passionate team and works with over 300 clients in any given year around her children. An entrepreneur at heart, Nic is a successful business educator and thought leader in Australia.

Nic is your everyday entrepreneur who had a dream and was not afraid of going for it. Her business is growing and up-scaling right before her eyes.

About Market Me Marketing

Email address
admin@marketmemarketing.com

Website
www.marketmemarketing.com

Blog
www.marketmemarketing.com/blog

Facebook
www.facebook.com/MMMarketing

Twitter
www.twitter.com/MarketMeMktg

Instagram
www.instagram.com/Marketmemarketing

PART 2

10K BOSS

A NON-PRESCRIBED JOURNEY

CAROLINE CARSWELL
Sound Advice

"The secret of change is to focus all your energy, not on fighting the old, but on building the new."

- Socrates, Philosopher

Their fingers circled an "O" around their mouth, and they glared at me with disgust.

In sign language, this "O" implies "oral deaf", a label given by many traditional signing deaf people to people like me – someone who was born deaf and has chosen to live in the mainstream world.

Who would have thought that I, a deaf person, was actually being labelled by the deaf community? Apparently in their eyes, it was abominable for a born-deaf person to confidently present as an oral deaf person who has successfully integrated with the mainstream community.

I found the whole situation rather ridiculous.

To top it off, this happened at a cochlear implant seminar in Dublin. I was there to learn more about cochlear implants, a hearing device that was not in my personal hearing toolkit for mainstream living at the time.

I didn't want to attract more attention, and possibly for the first time in my life I was glad that the digital hearing-aids in my ears were well hidden - despite their usefulness allowing born-deaf people to talk and live in the mainstream.

The realisation that my verbal deaf group of hearing-aid and cochlear implant wearers were treated like pariahs and being socially excluded was upsetting.

I walked away feeling like an outcast.

The year was 2007.

A Prescribed Life

Prescribing how one should live is such a strange concept. Why should someone be told how to live?

And how is one even given that level of authority to actually tell others what to do with their life?

And that is exactly what has been happening to verbal deaf people and their families.

I was among the first born-deaf children in Ireland to be mainstream-educated. I have worked hard all my life to participate in the mainstream community and achieved the goals that I set my mind to.

And guess what! I have lived my life without using any sign language.

Very often people have a preconceived idea about how deaf people should live regardless of their background. As a result, simply being a verbal deaf person can be seen as being a deviant in the deaf community. Choosing to use hearing technology and live in the mainstream community is also frowned upon.

I was growing more and more uncomfortable with the notion of a prescribed life, a life that was often designed by hearing people around signing deaf communities.

Recurring news headlines in Ireland in the mid-noughties were like adding wood to a dangerous fire, further fuelling my internal sense of injustice.

Stories of "deaf children being failed at school" and "deaf school-leavers reading like eight-year-olds" raised questions that auto-played in my head for days.

How did this education shortfall happen?

Were parents not being told about cochlear implants, available in Ireland since 1998?

Did their infants not get home-taught in spoken

language and reading skills before mainstream preschool, as my peer group did?

Perhaps school teachers were not being trained to include deaf pupils in mainstream classrooms and the digital tools they might use to learn?

I was both puzzled and very concerned.

Most of my childhood verbal deaf peer group were postgraduate-certified at the time, after completing full mainstream education with basic hearing-aids. Unlike us, today's deaf infants and children in Ireland had digital sound quality to live and learn in mainstream society with their families.

But deaf children were still failing at school.

So why were today's deaf children not flourishing?

Like I said, I was puzzled.

I found some answers in the prevailing Deaf culture and on the native deaf groups' websites.

Deaf Culture and Collective Denial

Written with a capital D, Deaf culture is the set of social beliefs, values and behaviours that are influenced by deaf people who use sign languages as their main means of communication.

While sign language plays an important role in the deaf community, it should not dominate the entire landscape. Unfortunately, the websites that hearing families and deaf people relied on for information in 2007 heavily prescribed Deaf culture with sign language as if signing was the only way.

No information was given about the 4 communication options for deaf infants or cochlear implants. And without being fully informed, a full generation of family futures was potentially at stake when a child was found to be profoundly deaf. Alarmingly, the informational websites even supported segregated education for deaf boys and girls.

What amazed me the most was that verbal deaf children and adults were excluded from these native deaf groups' websites. It would seem that this particular growing social group was completely invisible, and thus their needs were not being considered at all by the native deaf groups.

Were we excluded by the native deaf groups for being verbal, not using sign language and/or not participating in the signing deaf community?

So what if our verbal deaf identity meant we did not identify with signing Deaf culture?

What was so wrong that our mainstreamed lifestyles were different to those in the signing deaf community?

Isn't the diversity within us what contributes to the richness of our society?

A deaf person, like anyone in mainstream society, should be given the opportunity to explore options to fulfil their potential.

Options! That was all I asked for.

Not only was this collective denial about the diversity in the deaf population disturbing, this social exclusion also had a larger public health implication.

How were state policymakers and decision-makers to know that the signing Deaf culture was not always identified with by deaf individuals?

What was the impact of our hearing-deaf identity on our own future education and workplace prospects?

Something had to change in Ireland. But what

and how?

I had a few ideas.

What if I could redefine deaf role models?

What if I could make these new deaf role models visible to as many people as possible to guide on the ability of deaf infants and people with digital hearing-devices in the twenty-first century?

Could I use my corporate marketing skills and previous experience with Web 2.0 tools, targeting corporate clients for the public, educating them about a growing verbal deaf group who identified as being hard-of-hearing with devices?

What if I could tell the public about million-dollar deaf babies and share the important work of Mrs Devine, my childhood speech therapist?

Would that make a difference?

I WANTED to make a difference.

Million-Dollar Babies

The term million-dollar babies actually sounds rather glamorous. All babies are precious, and a description of being a "million-dollar" baby seems very fitting.

Unfortunately, that is not the case.

Million-dollar babies is actually a global term used to describe the overall lifetime costs associated with deaf babies, a figure relating to special education, lost wages and health complications if early intervention is absent.

According to Massachusetts Hearing Aid Coalition for Children's 2012 data, children who do not receive early intervention can incur an additional $420,000 apiece in education costs for state education agencies.

These figures clearly highlight the crucial importance and benefit of early intervention to deaf children's learning and development.

And Mrs Devine knew that.

My childhood speech therapist, Mrs Constance Devine, was a visionary. As a self-taught audiologist and speech therapist with general nursing training from the United Kingdom, Mrs Devine had the foresight and courage to break the norm and taught verbal deaf children in her clinic rooms at Dublin's Harcourt Street hospital.

Mrs Devine's journey began with a teaching position at St Mary's School for Deaf Girls at Cabra in Dublin in 1948. At the time, most deaf children in Ireland attended this campus to learn Irish sign language.

But the 4-year stay at this school had given Mrs Devine a different perspective. She found that a hearing environment was beneficial to deaf children. Instead of sending deaf babies from all over Ireland to Dublin to attend an institution, deaf babies could actually live with their families and attend their local mainstream schools after an infant verbal education with hearing-aids.

For her unconventional teaching ideology, Mrs. Devine was ostracised by the signing deaf community.

Unbeknown to everyone, her oral deaf education method is seen as the best practice today all over the world in countries like the United Kingdom, United States of America, Australia, New Zealand, South Africa, India and Sri Lanka.

Like many advocates, Mrs. Devine did not walk an easy path. Finding the first group of students and setting up a spoken language clinic in Dublin was hard. But the entrepreneur in her meant Mrs Devine did not give up.

Instead she sought moral support from doctors in her social network, travelled to the States in the late 1940s for research and observation into childhood oral deaf education and read books on deafness for teaching ideas.

Mrs Devine's big breakthrough came when an ear, nose and throat consultant at the National Children's Hospital at Harcourt Street in Dublin hired her to perform hearing tests on-site.

From this toehold base, she negotiated a fully-equipped speech-training clinic and began working with deaf children while optimising their residual hearing.

This approach was radical when the schools for the Deaf in Dublin believed that teaching deaf children to speak was not viable. Many parents at the time simply accepted the concept of their children being non-verbal, because that was what they were told by the specialist teachers in Dublin.

Although her unconventional teaching method drew heat from the Cabra teaching community for daring to be different, Mrs Devine's effort had enabled over 300 deaf children to become verbal between 1948 and 1992 and given them an opportunity to live in the hearing world, where they should be.

In 2004, a full 56 years after Mrs Devine advocated mainstream education for deaf children with hearing-aids and speech teaching, the Irish government decreed that all deaf children in Ireland should attend mainstream school where possible.

How personally satisfying that ruling must have been to her.

The inspirational and visionary Mrs Devine, who shaped my life and that of so many others, passed away in July 2016, aged 89.

The New Generation of Deaf Children

Despite the improvements over the years, astonishingly the same deaf education issues seem to persist in the twenty-first century. Perhaps it was time for me to continue Mrs Devine's work.

I wanted to change the notion that deaf people must live in a certain way. I wanted to empower today's deaf infants with options. I wanted to do this effectively and efficiently.

I found myself walking Mrs Devine's social entrepreneurial path.

I pitched my idea to Social Entrepreneurs Ireland about building a website as a resource for families and educators working with verbal deaf infants, children and students with hearing issues in mainstream education and workplaces.

My pitch apparently had potential. I was given an opportunity and EUR €5000 by Social Entrepreneurs Ireland to build a comprehensive website that could serve a wide range of key stakeholders.

It was exciting knowing I could make a difference with my idea. But I also found myself facing a universal problem that all social entrepreneurs face – passion alone does not put food on the table.

People asked how I could sustain myself without a regular income. But I was so committed to making a change that somehow I came up with strategies to support myself.

For example, I was willing to rent part of my house to students and young professionals. I also picked up a paid assignment that spring, digitising and rebuilding an online postgraduate course for a client.

The truth is I was so committed to the cause that if car parking space was available on our premises to let out, this option would have been explored too.

With all that, *irishdeafkids.ie* and the Irish Deaf Kids venture was born.

~

The Irish Deaf Kids website provided an opportunity for parent activists at grassroots level to connect and coordinate their advocacy efforts.

Reports of infants and children in Ireland waiting up to 5 years to get hearing aids from Ireland's public health service began coming in from families in Cork and Galway.

In science terms, this neurological emergency for deaf infants deepened with every month and level of hearing loss, bringing educational struggle from linguistic deprivation — which sadly happened among children born in Ireland before 2011. Case studies of verbal deaf children outside Ireland showed the folly of this needless situation.

Infants born overseas with profound hearing loss, who received digital hearing aids by 6 months old and/or a cochlear implant from 7 to 12 months old, were starting preschool with hearing peer-level spoken language and literacy skills to underpin their spoken language and educational progress.

Without infant access to hearing - and to spoken language - these deaf children in Ireland were at risk of lifelong social isolation and having their personal ability limited in school and in social contexts, even within their own family groups.

Knowing the native deaf community identified strongly with Deaf culture and had little incentive to alter a status quo to benefit the growing hearing-deaf community, I asked myself how to highlight this elephant in the room and to whom.

I decided that strategies involved both online and real-world outreach were required. So I began actively engaging core stakeholders including parents, educators, policymakers, technology firms and employers through conferences, workshops and seminars.

Our resource website opened a can of worms. My list of problems seemed to be growing by the day, requiring huge personal fortitude on my part.

The problem that topped the list was cash. Social enterprise or not, no one seems to be able to escape the perennial cash flow dilemma entrepreneurs face. Irish Deaf Kids was no different. While no money was spent on administrative work or office space, our initiatives such as stakeholder outreach through seminars, conferences and workshops required funding support.

Everywhere I looked, we needed money.

Growing the cash base for Irish Deaf Kids, however, was an energy-sapping and uphill push with shoestring budgets across every accounting category.

Luckily, I knew that building Irish Deaf Kids was not a solitary task. I was not afraid to seek help.

And in return, I received abundant assistance. For example, Irish Deaf Kids connected with a MBA student group at a Dublin university, who helped draft Irish Deaf Kids' business plan and gave us a strong start.

On-boarding several voluntary directors from the education, accounting, management and software sectors widened Irish Deaf Kids' internal talent. The chairman's charitable governance and compliance skills were a particular asset with Irish Deaf Kids' positioning as a disruptive entity right from the beginning, sparking possible opposition from the cultural deaf groups who preferred to maintain the status quo.

Slowly, with prudent financial management and a value-driven approach, Irish Deaf Kids built capital to finance its daily operations. I was also able to utilise my PR and marketing skills and reach parents, educators and policymakers through magazine and press articles, further advancing our work.

Social Entrepreneurs Ireland also proved to be a source of inspiration and help for Irish Deaf Kids beyond its initial seed funding of EUR €5000. In 2008, Irish Deaf Kids partnered with a fellow Social Entrepreneurs Ireland alumnus venture, Special Stories, to produce a children's book, a Birthday for Ben, for 5 to 8 year old children.

Royalties from the book helped fund Irish Deaf Kids' ongoing outreach activities, with online sales boosted by the move from Independent Television, a commercial TV network in the United Kingdom, to animate the book as a mobile phone app during 2010.

Forging Deeper Connections

Irish Deaf Kids was always about empowering families with deaf infants with accurate information and options. We constantly sought new ways to engage our communities.

For example, Irish Deaf Kids funded a short-term project with another Social Enterprise Ireland alumnus, who was a creative play facilitator at Dublin's Beaumont Hospital, the home to Ireland's national cochlear implant centre. The Learning Language Is Fun! Project sought to guide parents in the natural aural way to teach their children spoken language when hearing devices are first used. Through this project, we were able to start a dialogue with the parents of infants with cochlear implants about the services and approaches they could access.

Unbeknownst to me at the time, my personal challenges were yet to come.

I discovered I was losing my tiny bit of remaining hearing. My hearing fell sharply even with the best digital hearing aids available.

For months now I had been feeling fatigue – a tiredness not seen in my hectic student days, particularly after "seminar days" with various groups. It turned out my fatigue was the result of extra energy spent as I sought visual focus to compensate for hearing less and less.

Although cochlear implant surgery did not appeal, it was my only option for re-joining the world of partial sound. The sense of uncertainty was overwhelming. Questions swam in my head.

With a lifelong tie to Ireland's national cochlear implant centre after surgery, would I be able to work and live overseas?

What about my lifestyle like hillwalking and sports?

What would the sound quality be like?

While hearing-aids would be redundant after a cochlear implant surgery and would work with my remaining natural hearing when the device was inserted, after a lifetime with hearing-aids, I was not sure if I wanted a device in my head.

Like the verbal deaf individuals whose needs Irish Deaf Kids set out to serve, I was in need of quality information and invested many hours searching for details to make a decision.

I was once again reminded the importance of our work.

My eventual decision to go ahead with a cochlear implant surgery was swayed by 2 pieces of information I discovered. A post-surgery audiogram I found online from a contact whose hearing levels resembled mine eased my doubt about hearing quality associated with the implant. I was also encouraged by the fact that cochlear implant surgeries required less time to complete – 90 minutes per ear in contrast to 4 hours per ear in previous years.

Adapting to life with the new cochlear device brought me closer to Irish Deaf Kids and our goal. I was in fact using children's learning materials for sound and home-listening practice immediately after the cochlear device was activated.

The experience also strengthened my synergies with the parents of children in the Irish Deaf Kids network, who valued hearing-insights from a mainstreamed adult with a similar implant.

Many of their children, like myself, wore a digital

hearing-aid in their 'free' ear for binaural hearing with cochlear implants.

Nature gives two ears for a reason, and the aided ear in everyone's case was an 'anchor' to familiar sound for learning to hear with their newly-implanted ear.

When I started the Irish Deaf Kids journey, I genuinely did not expect that an implant would be acquired along the way. I now realised that, in fact, the experience was absolutely vital to the public outreach that the role required.

A Force of Disruption

We had always positioned Irish Deaf Kids as a disruptor within Irish society. But it gave us tremendous confidence when we could self-validate our social enterprise model during a 2015 business seminar delivered by one of the world's leading innovation experts and business strategists, Dr Trish Gorman.

Gorman believes focus and motivation are clear tenets of disruptive behaviours with solutions driven by tenacious problem-solvers who are visionaries, 'skunkworks' leaders and founders or entrepreneurs.

It was not hard to see that Irish Deaf Kids embodied those elements of disruptive innovation described by Gorman. Our quest to challenge the status quo, so set in stone by the native deaf groups, echoed Gorman's teaching – "Disruption breaks rules and challenges the very assumptions that provide guidance and direction to ongoing business."

Rather than maximising profit, Irish Deaf Kids set out to modernise Ireland's deaf sector and education from day 1 and as a disruptive entity, we achieved our goals by:

1. Creating visible deaf role models to transmit core values, coach on a new path of alignment and empowering others through shared objectives while conveying logic with data.
2. Achieving the disruptive effect of bilateral cochlear implants through the 2013 Happy New Ear campaign: Infants and children now hear speech in both ears with the obvious, related familial, social, educational and occupational benefits.
3. Communicating how eGovernment services can save capital by observing and emulating disruption models presented by rebel start-up entities and by change agents linking multiple sectors.

Listening to Gorman that day describing how "disruptive ideas are executed by provocateurs and expert critics, whose vision includes kickstarter tendencies and forming thought partnerships with others", I felt like arriving home after travelling full circle with Irish Deaf Kids.

In 2010, Irish Deaf Kids received Ireland's eGovernment Award (Education) for promoting cross-sector collaboration and cost-efficiency in the public sector.

What's Next?

Thinking back all those years ago, I was appalled by the collective denial within the Irish signing deaf community about the needs of verbal deaf groups.

Finally in 2015, Ireland's national TV broadcaster, RTE, recognised the diversity in the deaf population with a documentary on people who received cochlear implants.

Imagine how my verbal deaf peer group felt, to see people like ourselves on TV in Ireland - at last, after years of having to justify our speaking identity to every new person we met at college, in mainstream social groups, when travelling and in training sessions and workplaces.

As profoundly deaf people with speech in Ireland, we were invisible all these years.

Today's verbal deaf youngsters will not have to explain themselves or their personal identity to others. They will enjoy the freedom of choices and the ability to decide how they wish to live their life, without having to conform to a narrow societal perception of "how they should be".

In 2014, Irish Deaf Kids transitioned into Sound Advice. Today, Sound Advice is trading from Ireland and continues to receive international recognition as an innovative entity.

In February 2016, Sound Advice travelled to the United Nations in Austria. We were invited to speak about and exhibit on public infant hearing and speech services as a human rights issue after ranking in the Zero Project's top global-100 entities for inclusive education.

Sound Advice continues to enjoy opportunities to speak at public forums and innovation events, advocating for a fulfilling life for all deaf individuals and the social value of personal, lived experience.

From 2007 to 2014, Sound Advice's influencing (as Irish Deaf Kids) targeted a historic lack in Ireland's hearing and speech services that led to Ireland's Audiology Review in 2011, education policy for mainstreaming deaf children in 2011 and Health Service Executive-funded bilateral paediatric ear implants in 2013.

We are proud of what we have accomplished.

As Ralph Waldo Emerson puts it, "to be yourself in a world that is constantly trying to make you something else is the greatest accomplishment."

My prophet in the desert role was complete.

About Caroline Carswell

Caroline Carswell is a verbal cochlear implant wearer who does not use sign language. Among the first born-deaf children in Ireland to be mainstream-educated and without access support, Caroline graduated from Trinity College Dublin with an honours degree and two post-graduate certificates.

Caroline worked in Ireland and abroad for 15 years in digital publishing, journalism and corporate marketing before starting up Sound Advice.

Awards and Honours
- 2016: Zero Project, Top 100 Global Inclusive Education Entities
- 2010: Ireland's eGovernment Award (Education)
- 2007: Social Entrepreneurs Ireland Level 1 Award

About Sound Advice

Email address
hello@soundadvice.pro

Website
www.soundadvice.pro

Blog
sound-advice.ie/news

Facebook
www.facebook.com/SoundAdviceIreland

Twitter
www.twitter.com/soundadvice_pro

10K BOSS

PART 3

10K BOSS

MR ECONOMICS, I HAVE MADE IT!

ANDREW CONSTANTINE
CIO Cyber Security

"There will always be fear.
There will always be an excuse.
There will always be doubt.
There will always be that person who says don't.
There will always be a thousand and one reasons why you shouldn't do what you are thinking of doing.
Yet they are all irrelevant."

- Andrew Constantine

How were you supposed to feel when you were told that you were never going to make it in life?

I was not a bad kid. Unlike the rebellious drama one would find in Hollywood films, my high school life was not actually very exciting.

I was not a bad kid, I just did not like school. In fact, I only went to school for English and IT. Not because I was particularly interested in these 2 subjects either, but because I had great teachers who treated us like adults. In reality, I was an all F student.

"Andrew, if you don't knuckle down, you will never aspire to anything great in life. Continue the way you are going and you'll be working at McDonald's on minimum wage," said my Economics teacher one day.

Clearly, high school had failed me.

Life is 10% What Happens to You and 90% How You React to It

I hated school. It was a week before my High School Certificate exams that I realised I had a passion for IT. Though it was a little too late to drop out, so I stumbled through my final exams.

Years later I wished I had discovered my passion earlier, so I could dive into the world of IT and all its glory after Year 10 instead of forcing myself going through the motion of completing high school.

But I did discover my passion, and with the support of my parents, I began my adventure.

I found a position in the corporate world, being that 20-something-young-guy telling people what to fix and how to fix things. I was a little naive and very bold. My enthusiasm was not always appreciated by others.

Three years into it, it hit me.

Why am I here?

What am I doing here listening to these guys who have a sense of uninformed ignorance?

I handed in my resignation soon after. With the little amount of savings I had, I decided to start my own cyber security advisory firm. Then the *what-if* moment came.

What if I don't reach my goal?

What if I lose all my money?

What if something bad happens?

But then the question dwelled on me - *what if I don't?*

I decided that I needed to learn how to run a business. I wanted to learn it from people who had failed before and learn it in a short period of time – really, really fast.

So I spent $10,000 and enrolled myself in a business course. I was optimistic and full of excitement, living in the promises that everyone painted for me, believing that I was going to be a super star.

My optimism died a little after a year had gone by, and I still had not made a dollar. After all, starting a business was not all that easy.

But I was not a quitter.

I began looking for ways to win clients over. Patience and time played an important part in my growth strategy.

I took the time to understand what was happening in the industry and study what our competitors did not offer in response to industry changes. This gave me a point of difference.

I also took the marketing concept of split testing seriously. In the marketing world, to split test is to compare multiple versions of a campaign to work out the best version. Instead of only applying the concept to marketing, I took split testing to another level.

I split tested everything, and I meant everything.

From sales process to administrative task, I split tested everything.

Did it work? Why did it work?

Did it not work? Why didn't it work?

Those questions became my mantra.

Fast forward 7 years, it is a different scene.

As a young entrepreneur, I find myself mingling with technology executives from the top ASX 200 organisations in Australia.

What do I do? I successfully run a private cyber security advisory firm.

Mr Economics, you will be glad to know that McDonald's and minimum wage is nowhere in sight.

~

I discovered self-awareness very early on during my entrepreneurial journey.

I noticed that successful business owners and top executives have something in common. They are all highly self-aware individuals who have a deep understanding about their abilities.

Instead of perfecting a "weakness", many of these top performers have chosen to perfect what they are good at and the strengths in the area that they are passionate about.

This was my "a-ha" moment.

Throughout my schooling, I was constantly told to improve myself and to get better at something. I struggled to perfect my "weaknesses", because I had no interest or passion in those areas.

Understanding the "weaknesses versus strengths" concept gave me great comfort. It also explained why I excelled in running a private cyber security advisory firm despite failing miserably in high school.

Passion drives my ambition, tickles my curiosity and motivates me to be better.

The Power of Frustration

The world of technology can be very confusing. The amount of misinformation and misguided advice floating around was getting to me.

Keith Abraham, the world-leading thought leader once said, "when the why becomes clear, the how becomes easy."

My frustration about the misinformation and misguided advice in the IT industry was the starting point that defined my why and business niche. I realised I could help others traverse the complexity of the cyber world and help businesses avoid cyber attacks.

My well-defined why and my clear vision has shaped our marketing strategy. Instead of marketing our services to everyone, we were able to carve out our own target audience.

Today we have a very clear idea about our target audience. We work with organisations with an annual turnover between $20 Million to $300 Million and typically with companies who employ up to or around 500-1000 employees.

More importantly, my frustration also allowed me

to define my business mission – to educate over 10,000 technology leaders world-wide about cyber safety and security.

Who would have thought frustration could be this valuable?

Lessons

You are an entrepreneur, because you are not afraid of failure. More importantly, because you have this innate ability to learn from your mistakes and adapt your course for success.

As a young entrepreneur, I have my share of ups and downs and I have learned many great lessons. These are some of the key lessons I have learned along the way.

- **Business is a long game.**

If you think things will happen just because you deserve it or if you believe success will happen overnight, you are dead wrong

- **Don't work with everybody who wants to work with you.**

This may sound like a no brainer, but it is not as easy as it sounds. It contradicts the traditional thinking that the client is always right and that the client has the power. I made a conscious decision earlier on that our advisory firm will always focus on the quality rather than the quantity of clients. As such, there are times we actively decline smaller projects. This decision helps us better manage our resources as very often small projects demand similar level of resources and energy as big projects.

To determine which clients we should take on, I

always ask my prospective client this one question - what is that one thing you can bring to the table if we decide to work with you?

- **Systemise your business**

Believe it or not, multitasking does not work. As a business owner, you cannot possibly do 700 things at once. The practice of multitasking not only burns you out, the quality of your work suffers too. So I have implemented a 3-calendar system to systematically manage our time and resources at CIO Cyber Security.

The 3-Calendar System

Personal Calendar

This includes all things personal to you. Get everything out of your head and into your diary and online calendar. Haircuts, dental appointments, nail and manicures, spa treatments, physio, exercise, shopping - everything.

Internal Calendar

This has all our internal projects, team meetings, activities/games, seminars, conferences, events, holidays, training/education, performance reviews, 90 day action plans and more. These sessions are all blocked out in our calendar to avoid confusion and to improve efficiency. For example, if we generate a new lead who enquires about our services, everyone knows the only available option to schedule a session with me is on Wednesday.

Wednesday is the only time I do all my sales and marketing/business generating activities.

Client calendar

This is the calendar we supply to our clients. It contains events, seminars, conferences, webinars, networking events, Christmas events, strategy sessions and project management time frames/deadlines.

The 3-calendar system avoids "ad-hoc" situations and has allowed us to manage clients effortlessly.

- **Seriously, fail fast**

Many people talk about their million dollar dream. You only need to go on social media to understand the magnitude of this dreamy phenomenon.

The reality is if you want to be successful, you sure as hell need to know what you are doing and accept the fact that failure is a constant in the life of your entrepreneurial quest.

In fact, you need mistakes and failures to guide and reassure you that you are still on the right path - as long as you "fail and fail fast". The quicker you can understand what went wrong, the quicker you can learn how to move past it.

One way to ensure you can fail and fail fast is by split testing everything regularly. At CIO Cyber Security, we have a 90-day split test cycle. We split test all aspects of our operation quarterly, from technology to operations to administrative tasks. As the Director of our company, I benefit from early warnings using split testing before an issue escalating into a significant problem and causing havoc.

I remember how shocked I was with one particular split test result. We were running direct mail campaigns to engage 150 technology leaders. Despite all the effort, we only had one person responded. We then tested a different sales process by hosting small and intimate breakfast forums, which yielded a much better response.

What this split test had shown us was that people didn't want to be sold to.

Guided by our split test data, now CIO Cyber Security runs small but intimate events. We purposely limit our guest attendance to 15 to 30 technology leaders per session. This gives us a better engagement rate and a meaningful opportunity to talk about all things cyber security.

- **Surround yourself with like-minded, passionate and driven people**

If you hang around 5 confident people, you could be the 6th. If you hang around intelligent people, you could even grow your intelligence. If you hang around millionaires, you could possibly be the next millionaire. But one thing for sure, if you hang around idiots, you will be an idiot. And if you hang around 5 broke people, you'll likely be broke.

Perhaps it is oversimplified, but the concept is fairly self-explanatory. Do I need to go on?

Back to the Beginning

So back to where I started, how were you supposed to feel when you were told that you were never going to make it in life?

You ignore the comment and you move on. You

look within yourself to discover your deepest passion. You then take that passion, make something meaningful and share it with the big wild world.

About Andrew Constantine

When it comes to protecting your business from cyber threats, Andrew Constantine is one person you definitely want in your corner.

With years of experience in information security and an intuitive grasp of how online attackers think, Andrew is one of Australia's leading experts in keeping your business's vital data safe.

Before finding his passion in cyber security, life was a struggle. With very little interest in school and a report card filled with Fs, Andrew was a failure to most people.

Lucky for Andrew, he discovered his passion for IT and has since built a successful business, offering specialist knowledge and advice in the area of cyber security.

About CIO Cyber Security

Email address
info@CIOCyberSecurity.com.au

Website
www.CIOCyberSecurity.com.au

Blog
https://TheCIOSolutionBook.com.au

10K BOSS

www.ingramcontent.com/pod-product-compliance
Lightning Source LLC
Chambersburg PA
CBHW072108290426
44110CB00014B/1865